ORLAND PARK PUBLIC LIBRARY

3 1315 00442 8905

 P9-CCU-168

DISCARD NOV 2006

ORLAND PARK PUBLIC LIBRARY
14921 S. RAVINIA AVENUE
ORLAND PARK, ILLINOIS 60462
708-349-8138

Sandra Markle

Little Lost Bat

ORLAND PARK PUBLIC LIBRARY

Illustrated by
Alan Marks

⌒ Charlesbridge

With love for my mother, Dorothy Haldeman—S. M.

To Preston Primary School—A. M.

Acknowledgments

Sandra Markle would like to thank Barbara French, Bat Conservation International, and Amanda Lollar, founder and president of Bat World Sanctuary, for sharing their expertise and enthusiasm. A special thank you to Skip Jeffery for his loving support throughout the creative process.

Text copyright © 2006 by Sandra Markle
Illustrations copyright © 2006 by Alan Marks
All rights reserved, including the right of reproduction in whole or in part in any form.
Charlesbridge and colophon are registered trademarks of Charlesbridge Publishing, Inc.

Published by Charlesbridge
85 Main Street
Watertown, MA 02472
(617) 926-0329
www.charlesbridge.com

Library of Congress Cataloging-in-Publication Data
Markle, Sandra.
   Little lost bat / Sandra Markle ; illustrated by Alan Marks.
      p. cm.
   Summary: "Chronicles the early life of an orphaned Mexican free-tailed bat, from its birth to its adoption by a new mother. Includes back matter about bats"—Provided by publisher.
   ISBN-13: 978-1-57091-656-4; ISBN-10: 1-57091-656-X (reinforced for library use)
1. Tadarida brasiliensis—Infancy—Juvenile literature. I. Marks, Alan, 1957– ill. II. Title.
QL737.C54M37 2006
599.4'9—dc22   2005019619

Printed in China
(hc) 10 9 8 7 6 5 4 3 2 1

Illustrations done in watercolor, pen, and pencil on Daler Bloxworth paper
Display type and text type set in Elroy and Fairfield
Color separations by Chroma Graphics, Singapore
Printed and bound by Jade Productions
Production supervision by Brian G. Walker
Designed by Susan Mallory Sherman

It's a warm June day in central Texas.
And high on the domed roof of Bracken Cave—
so far from the cave mouth that it's almost
too dark for shadows—
one little female Mexican free-tailed bat
clings tightly to the ceiling
with her toes and wing claws
poked into cracks.
Then she curls her body into a hammock shape.
It's time for her baby to be born.

Even though the rock cave is as huge
as a cathedral, it's steamy hot
from the body heat of
millions of female bats
packed close together.
And it's shockingly
noisy
from so many bat voices.
The sounds are made even louder by echoes
bouncing
off the cave's walls, ceiling, and floor.

Yet all the while she labors,
the little female calls,
CH-CH-CH!
CH-CH-CH!
CH-CH-CH!
No matter that it's noisy all around her.
She's only calling to one listener,
her baby.

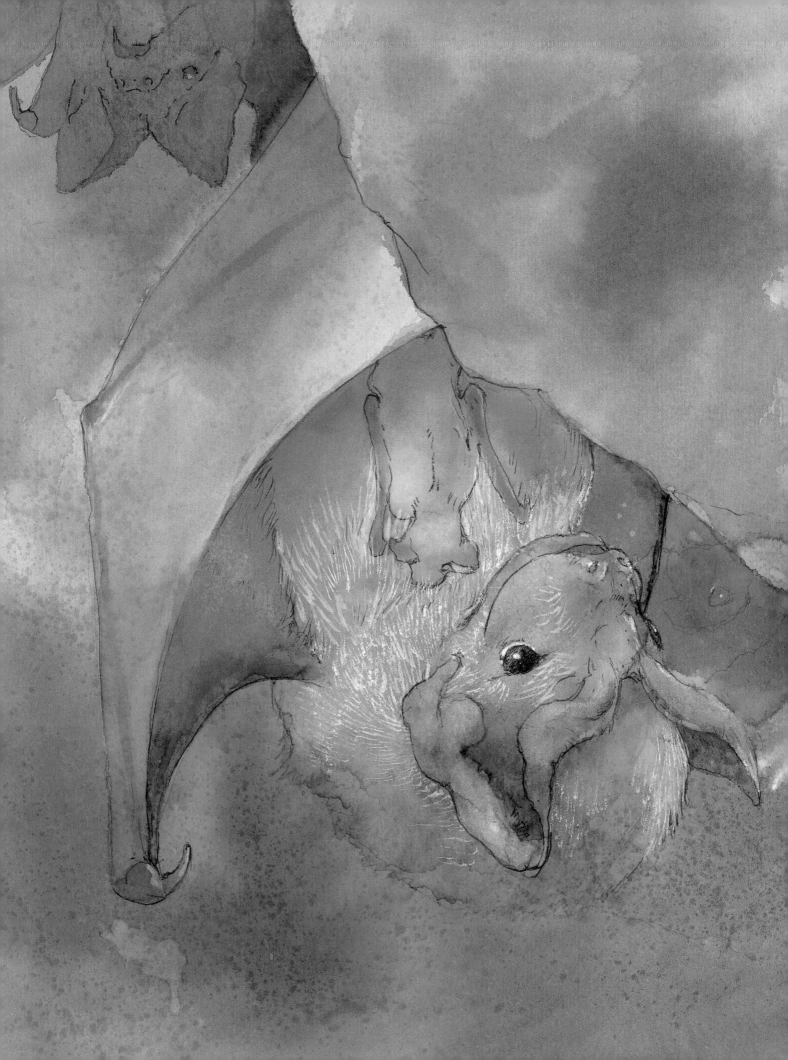

And the instant he's born—
naked-pink and tiny as a peanut in its shell—
she folds up her tail membrane to keep him from falling
down,
down,
down
to the waiting, hungry beetles
on the cave floor.

Then the little bat,
nudged by his mother,
crawls up onto her chest,
clinging to her fur
with tiny hooked claws.
There he finds a nipple,
and, tucked beneath her wing,
he nurses.

During the day, the little bat's mother
is only as far away as her roost.
She rests among all of the other mothers.
And she flies back a few times a day to her little bat
to let him nurse.
The babies huddle together
and wait for their mothers to return.
A snake lurking at the entrance
crawls across the cave ceiling
and snags a baby bat for dinner.
Still, there is safety among such great numbers.

But as the day ends,
some inner sense lets the mother know it's time
to leave the cave and hunt.
With no partner to help her,
she has to feed herself
as well as her baby.
So the mother bat
joins the millions of female bats
racing out of the cave.

The cloud of bats
explodes into the twilight
like dark fireworks.
Hawks hunting in the sky catch a few of the mothers.

442 8905

The females, forced to spread out to start hunting,
zip this way and that.
Each nursing mother needs to eat
nearly her weight in insects
before the night is through.

ORLAND PARK PUBLIC LIBRARY

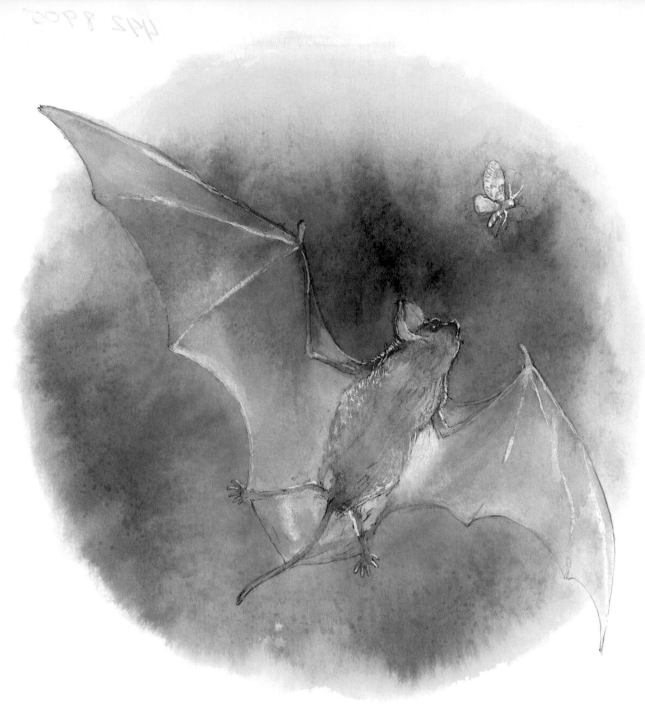

Flapping hard,
the little bat's mother shoots bursts
of high-pitched sounds from her mouth.
And she listens
with big ears, turning to catch the echoes
bouncing back.
Analyzing these in a flash,
she homes in on a moth.

Slap! She sweeps her prey
toward her body with a wing stroke.
Next, she scoops it up,
using her tail membrane like a catcher's mitt,
and ducks her head
to gulp down the bug.
Hunting this way, she eats her fill of
moths, beetles, and a few mosquitoes.

But the mother bat never flies too far
from the cave.
Between courses of her insect feast,
she goes home
to the rocky roost
where she left her little bat.

The minute she lands,
dozens of hungry,
naked, pink baby bats
push,
shove,
and crawl over each other,
trying to reach her.
Each cries loudly,
pleading to be fed.

Among the crowd of babies,
the little bat listens for his mother's call:
CH-CH-CH!
CH-CH-CH!
CH-CH-CH!
And hearing it, he calls, too:
Sh-sh-sh!
Sh-sh-sh!
Sh-sh-sh!
At the sound of his soft call, his mother crawls
from crack to crack across the ceiling
through the pack of crying baby bats.
His scent—and her own scent rubbed on him—
helps her find her little bat.

She covers him
with her furry warmth.
And snug
between the smooth rock
and his mother,
the little bat
tips his head back, finds a nipple,
and nurses.

The days pass this way,
one after the other,
for just over a week.
The mother leaves the little bat
while she hunts and sleeps.
In between, she cuddles him
and lets him nurse.
So the little bat grows bigger,
safe in the big cave under his mother's care.
And he starts to grow his first fur coat.

Then one night,
the mother bat's hunting flight
takes her skimming past
a tall oak tree.
Suddenly,
just as she catches a moth,
a shadow high up among the leafy branches
moves.
When the shadow takes flight
on great pumping wings,
the moonlight reveals
it's a barn owl.

Fast and silent,
the owl swoops in hot pursuit.

Always alert to danger,
the mother bat quickly senses the owl.
She flaps hard and turns sharply.
But the owl's big black eyes on its ghost-white face
track her every move.
And the owl chases after her.

Then, plunging through the night,
the owl thrusts out its long legs
and spreads toes tipped with slender claws
to snatch the mother bat
out of the air.

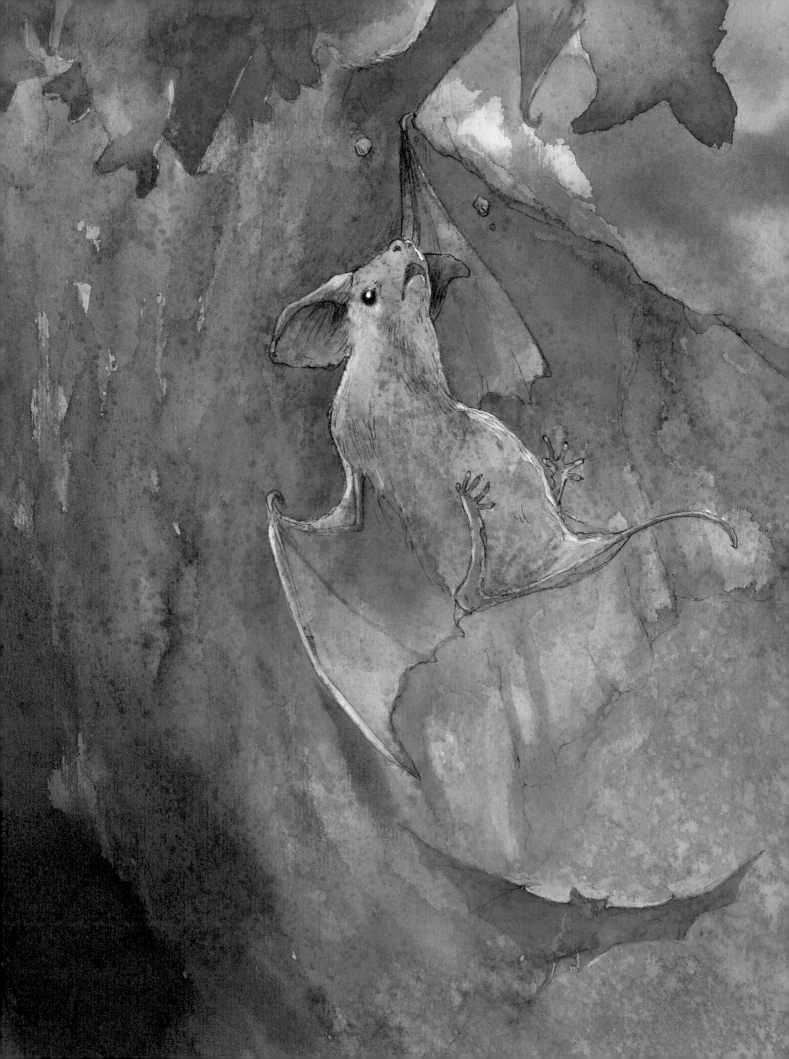

That night the little bat waits
and waits
and waits.
But his mother doesn't come back to him.
Each time he sees a female land nearby,
he scrambles toward her.
But each female pushes him away
to claim another baby.
Not one of them is his mother.

Once, when he's pushed,
the little bat slips.
But he grabs onto the rocky ceiling just in time
to keep from tumbling
down,
down,
down
to the waiting, hungry beetles
on the cave floor.

The little bat cries for his mother
and crawls across the cave ceiling
searching for her
until—exhausted—he sleeps.
When he wakes up, hungrier than ever,
he searches for her again.
For three days and nights, he searches
and cries for her to find him.

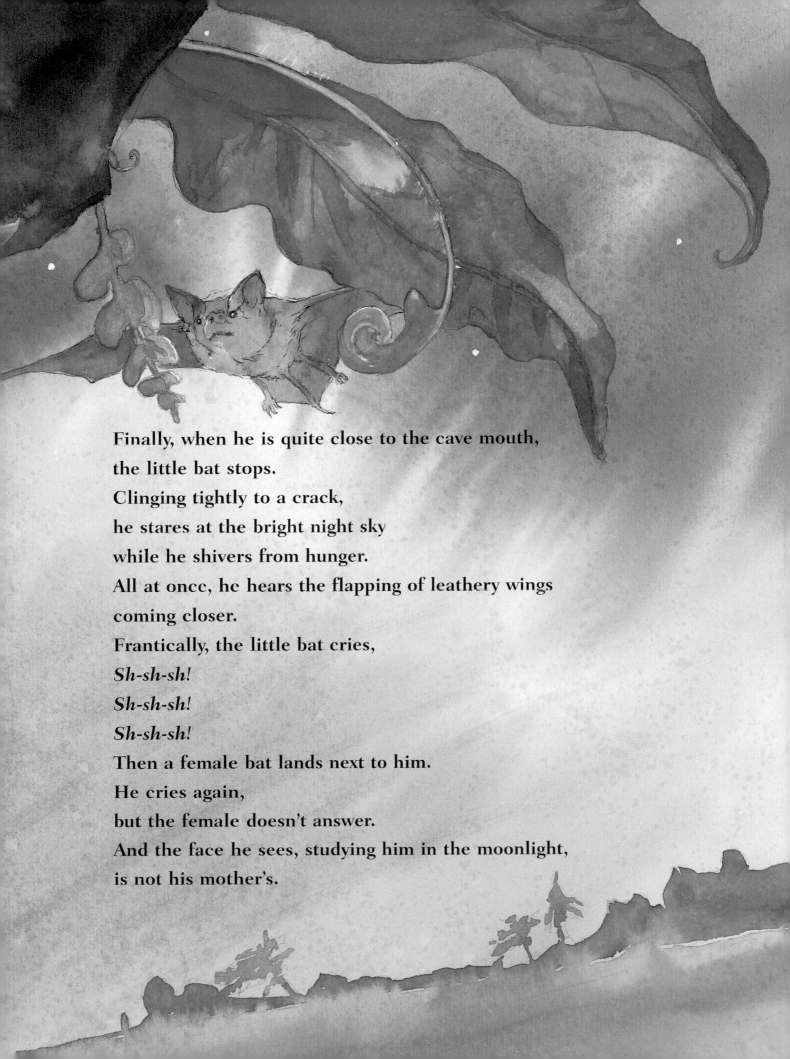

Finally, when he is quite close to the cave mouth,
the little bat stops.
Clinging tightly to a crack,
he stares at the bright night sky
while he shivers from hunger.
All at once, he hears the flapping of leathery wings
coming closer.
Frantically, the little bat cries,
Sh-sh-sh!
Sh-sh-sh!
Sh-sh-sh!
Then a female bat lands next to him.
He cries again,
but the female doesn't answer.
And the face he sees, studying him in the moonlight,
is not his mother's.

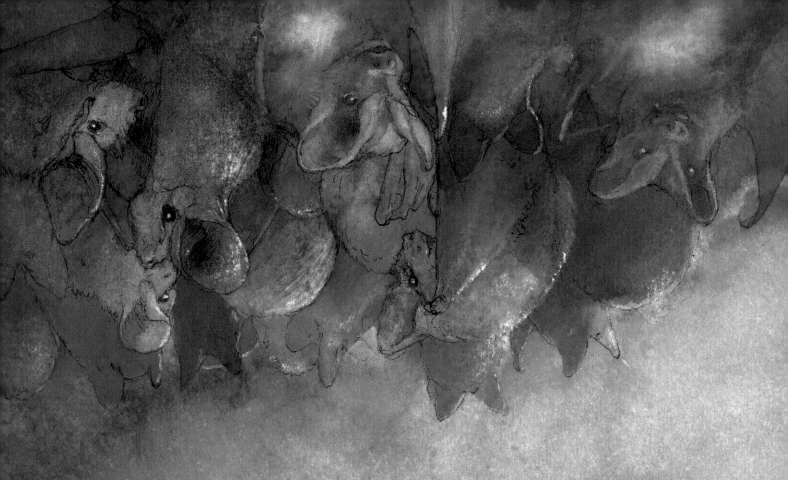

For three days,
this mother bat has been searching, too,
for the baby she left at
almost exactly this spot.
But she has never been able to find her baby.
Now, the female bat calls,
CHU-CHU-CHU!
CHU-CHU-CHU!
CHU-CHU-CHU!

It's not his mother's call,
but the little bat answers her anyway.

Instead of pushing him away,
she covers him
with her furry warmth, holds him snug,
and lets him nurse.
And all the while,
she keeps on calling softly just to him,
CHU-CHU-CHU!
CHU-CHU-CHU!
CHU-CHU-CHU!

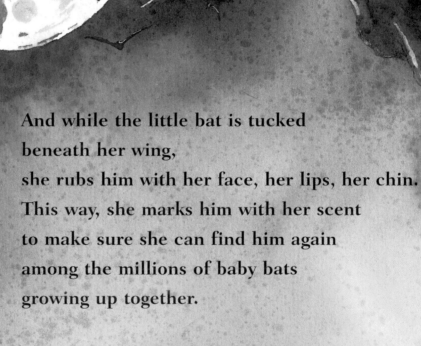

And while the little bat is tucked
beneath her wing,
she rubs him with her face, her lips, her chin.
This way, she marks him with her scent
to make sure she can find him again
among the millions of baby bats
growing up together.

Safe with his new mother,
the little bat calls once more, just for her,
Sh-sh-sh!
Sh-sh-sh!
Sh-sh-sh!
And falls asleep.

Author's Note:

Scientists are still investigating Mexican free-tailed bats. While they agree on many of the facts about how these bats live and hunt, they are still studying how the females raise their young. Tissue tests show as many as 10 percent of all Mexican free-tailed bat mothers aren't the genetic mothers of the babies they're nursing, so many researchers believe some orphan babies get adopted. While research continues, the hope is that some lost baby bats do share this story's happy ending.

Resources

Bat World www.batworld.org
Kids' pages include bat facts, games, and information on how to adopt a bat, helping the nonprofit organization Bat World rehabilitate injured and orphaned bats. Adoption sponsors receive the adopted bat's photo and personal history, an adoption certificate, and a year's subscription to their newsletter.

Bat Conservation International www.batcon.org
A camera provides live views of a real bat colony. Get directions for building a bat house that will invite bats to live close to you, and more.

Earle, Ann. *Zipping, Zapping, Zooming Bats.* New York: HarperCollins, 1995. An easy-to-read overview of bats, including how they help people and how people can help them.

Markle, Sandra. *Outside and Inside Bats.* New York: Walker, 2004. Investigates many different kinds of bats while learning how a bat's body functions and why bats behave the way they do.

Wood, Lily. *Bats.* New York: Scholastic, 2001. An easy-to-read text that offers an introduction to where bats live, what they eat, how they find food, and more.

Mexican free-tailed bats are amazing!

- Bats fly with their hands! A bat's wing is like skin stretched over a hand with really long fingers.

- Bracken Cave, close to Austin, Texas, is the summer home of more than 20 million Mexican free-tailed bats. This is a nursery cave, meaning that the only residents are female bats and their babies.

- The floor of Bracken Cave is covered with guano—bat wastes—several feet (about one meter) thick. The beetles and other animals that live in the guano will attack, overpower, and eat any baby bats that fall to the cave floor.

- Baby Mexican free-tailed bats can fly when they are six to eight weeks old.

- Bat babies weigh about a third as much as their mother at birth. That's like a human mother giving birth to a baby weighing about 40 pounds (18 kilograms).

ORLAND PARK PUBLIC LIBRARY